TABLE OF CONTENTS

CHAPTER ONE

INTRODUCTION

The Preamble to the Constitution of the United States provides a mandate for the union of

the United States "to insure domestic tranquility and provide for the common defense."[1]

Throughout our nation's history, the brunt of that mission has fallen on the Army and other

Services now within the Department of Defense. Over the years, U.S. forces have conducted a

wide range of tasks in defense of the U.S. homeland, such as defeating the Indians to conquer the

North American landmass, quelling the Whiskey Rebellion of 1794, or defeating British attacks

on coastal cities during the War of 1812.[2] Since 1812 (and until most recently), the U.S. has been

relatively void of physical catastrophes and bloody destruction.[3] Consequently, homeland

security has had little attention or priority in U.S. national security policy.

Today, however, the developing global economy, the revolution in information

technologies, and other advances of technology have added new dimensions to the homeland

security paradigm. Namely, the changing environment has vastly altered the warfighting

strategies of many U.S. adversaries. Recognizing the futility of attempting parity with U.S.

military forces in major theater war, many actors have instead turned to the acquisition of long-

range missiles, weapons of mass destruction (WMD), international and domestic terrorism, and

cyber attacks to strike out against American symbols of freedom and power in the world.[4]

---

[1] "Constitution of the United States, September 17, 1787" in Robert K. Wright, Jr., and Morris J. MacGregor, Jr., eds., *Soldier-Statesmen of the Constitution* (Washington, DC: Center of Military History, United States Army, 1987), 214.

[2] Antulio J. Echevarria II, *The Army and Homeland Security: A Strategic, Perspective* (Carlisle Barracks, PA: Strategic Studies Institute, 2001), 1.

[3] John J. Hamre, "A Strategic Perspective on U.S. Homeland Defense: Problem and Response," in *"...to insure domestic Tranquility, provide for the common defense..."*, Max G. Manwaring, ed., (Carlisle Barracks, PA: Strategic Studies Institute, 2000), 12.

[4] Eric V. Larson and John E. Peters, *Preparing the U.S. Army for Homeland Security: Concepts, Issues and Options* (Santa Monica, CA: RAND, 2001), 1.

Recent events both at home and abroad have demonstrated the emergence of this current complex threat situation and highlight America's growing vulnerability. The list below emphasizes some of the most significant, recent terrorist events:[5]

- The World Trade Center bombing in 1993

- The bombing of the Murrah Federal Building in Oklahoma City in 1995

- The 1995 use of nerve agents against the Tokyo subway system

- The Centennial Park bombing in Atlanta during the 1996 Olympics

- The bombing in June 1996 of the Al Khobar barracks in Saudi Arabia

- The simultaneous attacks in August 1998 on U.S. embassies in Nairobi and Dar es Salaam

- The attacks on the World Trade Center and Pentagon on September 11, 2001

These events should have been "wake up" calls to American leaders of the immediate threat to U.S. national security at home. However, it has taken the tragic events of the September 11, 2001 terrorist attacks on the World Trade Center and the Pentagon to finally get political leaders and American citizens to voice concern over the fragile security that many had presumed to exist on the American homeland for so long.

The seriousness of this latest incident beckons us to ask what steps the U.S. government should take to prevent future tragedies like these from happening. Better intelligence gathering on state and non-state actors with hostile intent and commensurate capabilities to act is one way; another is more effective information (warfare) campaigns to thwart the actions of potential aggressors. Regardless of the effectiveness of these first measures, the U.S. must continue to improve its ability to prepare for, prevent, deter, and respond to attacks on the homeland. Before the events of September 11, two Presidential Decision Directives (PDD) provided policy

---

[5] Ibid., 2.

guidance for combating terrorism and WMD (PDD 39 and 62).[6] The policy places lead agency responsibility with the Department of Justice (DOJ) and assigns responsibilities of crisis management and consequence management to the Federal Bureau of Investigations (FBI) and Federal Emergency Management Agency (FEMA), respectively. DOD only plays a supporting role to these agencies. Is this the best way to organize Federal Government resources to help local authorities? Some think not. Given it's inherent capability and organizational structure to respond to national security interests around the world, many suggest an increased role for DOD in homeland security–especially Army units—who have the forces most capable of responding to biological and chemical terrorism, our greatest threat.[7] The terrorist attacks of September 11, 2001 might also suggest that few organizations in the U.S. other than those assets organic to DOD could indeed provide such an immediate internal defense of our nation in response to terrorism.

The myriad of issues–legal, historical, and social—as well as the list of proponents on the varying sides of the matter, regarding employment of military assets in support of national emergencies within the U.S., is extensive. For one, the military does not particularly care to take any kind of lead role in homeland defense, citing both legal and practical considerations involved.[8] Secondly, and perhaps most importantly, the *Posse Comitatus* Act limits how the nation can use Armed Forces in response to domestic threats. Originally passed in 1878, with intent to end the use of federal troops to police state elections in former Confederate states, the *Posse Comitatus* Act specifically prohibits the military from enforcing civil criminal law within the U.S.[9] There are several exceptions to the law, but in terms of responding to homeland emergencies, *Posse Comitatus* severely limits the involvement of regular military forces during

---

[6] The White House, *PDD-39*, "U.S. Policy on Counter-terrorism," June 21, 1995 [on-line]; available from http://www.fas.org/irp/offdocs/pdd39.htm; Internet; accessed 27 March 2002; and The White House, *PDD-62*, "Protecting Against Unconventional Threats to the Homeland and Americans Overseas," May 22, 1998 [on-line]; available from (web address); Internet; accessed 27 March 2002.

[7] Russell Howard, "Chemical and Biological Terrorism: Political Hype or Bona Fide Post-Cold War Threat?" in *"...to insure domestic Tranquility, provide for the common defense...",* Max G. Manwaring, ed., (Carlisle Barracks, PA: Strategic Studies Institute, 2000), 115-116.

[8] Ibid., 119-120.

[9] Larson and Peters, 243.

federal emergencies, even when they may be the most adequate organization to respond to such incidences.[10]

Given the current threat situation, it may be time to review and perhaps revise the *Posse Comitatus* Act. This monograph approaches homeland security as a strategic issue, examining DOD's role and the viability of the *Posse Comitatus* Act when viewed through the rubric of the current (and future) threat environment. By exploring DOD's historic role in the defense of the U.S. homeland and the advent of the *Posse Comitatus* Act—its history, application, and weakening over the last couple of decades—the monograph seeks to determine if regular Armed Forces (and specifically the active Army) should play a more significant role in the homeland security mission.

The evaluation criteria will follow the "FAS" test model, as proposed in Joint Pub 3.0, Appendix B (The Estimate Process), which assesses the feasibility, acceptability, and suitability of strategy to ensure that elements of U.S. national security are not in danger.[11] Feasibility is an assessment of the strategic concept (ways) given the resources available (means). Determining feasibility involves art and science. We determine acceptability by comparing the resources required (means) and the benefits to be achieved (ends). The means must be consistent with the law of war and politically supportable. A military objective is suitable if, when achieved, it leads to a desired political or national security objective.[12]

In the succeeding chapters, this monograph argues that given the current threat environment, the *Posse Comitatus* Act is one of several factors limiting the development and execution of effective homeland defense doctrine in America. Amongst several options for change, it argues that at a minimum, the Act should be revised to facilitate the full use of DOD capabilities for domestic defense. The monograph contends that in order to maximize the

---

[10] Howard, 115-122.
[11] Joint Chiefs of Staff, *Joint Pub 3.0, Doctrine for Joint Operations* [CD-ROM] (Washington, D.C., 2001).
[12] Ted Davis, "Evaluating National Security Strategy and National Military Strategy," Reprinted in US Command and General Staff College, *C500 Fundamentals of Operational Warfighting*, (Fort Leavenworth,

Nation's ability to prepare for, prevent, deter, and respond to attacks on the homeland, DOD must consider expansion of the Army as part of its transformation efforts and include in the Army mission an increased role in homeland defense tasks.

Chapter Two of the monograph begins with a brief history of DOD's role in the defense of the American homeland. Building upon this historical view, the monograph will then focus on the emergence of U.S. Armed Forces as *posse comitatus*, and the creation of the Posse Comitatus Act as an evolution of the Nation's long-standing fear of standing army involvement in domestic affairs. This Chapter acknowledges the significance of the *Posse Comitatus* Act in American history, but posits that in today's strategic and domestic environment in the U.S. the Act has limited application or impact.

Chapter Three will explore the broader context in which U.S. homeland security policy is developed by discussing its framework. Then with both the historical perspective and current doctrinal framework as a backdrop, the monograph will explore the growing irrelevance of the Posse Comitatus Act by focusing on changes to the Act brought on by growth of the military involvement in the War on Drugs in the 1980s, and expanding use of military forces in other domestic support operations.

Chapter Four examines the domestic policy of three allied nations—Israel, Canada, and the United Kingdom—to explore how their planning and execution of domestic security tasks compares with and may lend to future U.S. policy. This discussion highlights the fact that each nation, being very experienced in terrorism and domestic violence, has clearly defined procedures for employment of military forces for domestic security matters. It also highlights several options for use of armed forces as lead agency for domestic crises, insights into interagency coordination during crises, and lastly, the importance of unity of command.

The recommendations and conclusions provided in Chapter Five identifies actions that the U.S. can take to legitimize use of Armed Forces in domestic operations, with or without *Posse*

KS: Command and General Staff College, 2000), L1-E-1,2.

Comitatus. It also provides several (not necessarily new) ideas on how the U.S. can provide better domestic security overall in the short and long term. The conclusion succinctly summarizes the necessity for change.

CHAPTER TWO

HISTORY OF DOD'S ROLE IN HOMELAND DEFENSE

Homeland Defense and its Origins in America

The historical precedent for military involvement in homeland defense originates in the very foundation of the colonies in the North American wilderness by English settlers in the 1600s. In the earliest days of English settlement on the continent, of necessity, the colonists created militia systems to defeat the native Indians, pirates and European rivals (Spaniards, Frenchmen, Hollanders) who had already laid claim to the territories they intended to inhabit.[13] All of the colonies (except Quaker Pennsylvania) adopted a system of universal military service, requiring all able-bodied males, normally men between 16 and 60 years of age, to become part-time soldiers. Each was required to own a weapon, train with neighbors, report for periodic muster or training days, and be on-call to repel attacks against their colony.[14] In these early times, colonial militia tended to be very diverse, but overall, the militia was a local institution, devoted to a local defense function. They typically served more effectively as a local police force or as a standby *posse comitatus*.[15] Militia "preserved the domestic peace, protected propertied and privileged colonists from the disadvantaged elements within society, and quelled movement against the established political order."[16]

---

[13] Alan R. Millett & Peter Maslowski, *For the Common Defense: A Military History of the United States of America.* (New York, NY: The Free Press, 1994), 1-2.

[14] Gregory J. W. Urwin, "The Army of the Constitution: The Historical Context," in *"…to insure domestic Tranquility, provide for the common defense…"*, Max G. Manwaring, ed., (Carlisle Barracks, PA: Strategic Studies Institute, 2000), 28.

[15] *Posse Comitatus* is a domestic law term. *Black's Law Dictionary* defines *posse comitatus* as: "the power or force or the county. The entire population of a country above the age of fifteen, which a sheriff may summon to his assistance in certain cases as to aid him in keeping the peace, in pursuing and arresting felons, etc." (See Larson and Peters, 243).

[16] Millett and Maslowski, pg. 7. In the South, colonies merged their slave patrols and militia together to form an internal police force to recover fugitive slaves and to suppress slave insurrections. In the North (New England), militias were often converted into civil police by combining it with night watches. Along with local defense functions, some colonies formed "scout" or "ranger" units that patrolled the frontier to disrupt attacks on their colonies (See Millett and Maslowski, 10).

With expansion of the colonies, dependence on the militia system lessened, as colonial governments replaced concern for protecting their own properties and maintaining the status quo with the more important task of protecting their frontiers. A volunteer militia persisted with a strictly local defense focus, but instead of sole reliance on the militia for defense, Colonists enlisted the service of paid, semi-regulars called Provincials. Provincials were voluntary enlistees or draftees from the militia who served for a campaign season or one year. During the series of European conflicts for colonial dominance in America called the Colonial Wars (1689-1763), Provincials (along with British Regulars) were integral in building forts and outposts in strategic locations to improve security between the colonies, influencing the natives, and expanding the colonial frontiers.[17] Most notably, Provincial troops were integral to the British Redcoat's defeat of the French in the Seven Years' War (1755-1763), which rid the Thirteen Colonies of French influence.[18] The Colonial Wars had a significant effect on early homeland defense doctrine. First, they validated the colonists' system—the militia—to defend themselves. Second, they had a nationalizing impact, both in terms of the various militias coming together and for the local governments working together. Third, the wars began a distinct separation from England.[19]

The Colonists had a great prejudice against using standing armies in defense of their territories, which was rooted in British political and constitutional thought. In England, the future pioneers witnessed the struggle between Parliament and the Crown over control of the British army in the 1600s. They were made to pay annual taxes to support the army, and there developed the idea that the military was a grave source of power, utterly despotic, and therefore a threat to liberty. In the colonies, the growing incidents of civil-military friction between British troops and colonials, such as suppression of riots, looting, and destroying property, served as a constant reminder of the very oppression and crude authoritarianism they had experienced in England, and desperately wanted to avoid. Through the Colonial Wars, Americans increasingly began to

---

[17] Ibid., 33.
[18] Urwin, 29-31.

8

associate an American standing army with the same oppression that could potentially overthrow U.S. civil power. The Boston Massacre of April 1770 was the event that permanently embedded the prejudice against standing armies into the American political tradition, affecting military defense policy in the U.S. homeland for several generations.[20]

Following the Boston Massacre, the newly formed Second Continental Congress adopted the first professional military system—The Continental Army—for its declared war against England. Like the Provincials, the soldiers of the Continental Army initially served only one-year enlistments. After near defeat in the later months of 1776, Congress sought a recruitment policy to make the Army a band of long-term regulars, which lasted throughout the war. During the American Revolution, the newly formed Continental Army served alongside the mobilized militiamen. The Continental Army won America her freedom; the militia, however, had a mixed battlefield record, at best. In sum, the Revolution, helped prove that the militia was unreliable, inefficient, and incapable of providing adequate security for the North American territories.[21] Nevertheless, after the Continental victory in the American Revolution, Congress quickly reduced the Continental Army to a single regiment and once again put the defense of its frontiers predominantly in the hands of the minutemen. This led to a stirring national debate regarding the nation's requirements for common defense.

Even as the debate developed, Congress disbanded the Continental Army in June 1784 and replaced it with a 700-man force classified as the 1st American Regiment. The Regiment, a combination of soldiers taken from four northern state militias, was more a constabulary than an army, and was assigned duty in small detachments along the Ohio Valley. In April 1785, amid unrelenting violence from Indian tribes in the Western frontier, Congress converted the regiment

---

[19] Millett and Maslowski, 45-46.

[20] Richard H. Kohn, *Eagle and Sword: The Beginnings of the Military Establishment in America*, (New York, NY: The Free Press, 1975), 3-6. The Boston Massacre was a riot which broke out between Massachusetts militia and British Regulars in 1770. After continued escalation of civil-military friction, British Regulars killed five civilians in the streets. The citizens of Boston retaliated (See Kohn, 5-6).

[21] Ibid., 9.

into a regular corps, by extending the length of service from one to three years. In subsequent years, this force proved unable to provide for any kind of common defense of the American frontier. In a seven-year period, 1783 to 1790, over 1,500 Kentuckians were tragically murdered by Indian raiders. During the same period, Shay's Rebellion in the fall of 1786, threatened domestic tranquility in the country's populated areas, and though crushed, provoked widespread disillusionment and convinced Congress that something needed to be done to strengthen the country's common resolve as well as protect the nation against all types of external and internal threats.[22] These events set the stage for the Constitutional Convention held in Philadelphia and led to the revision of the Articles of Confederation into the U.S. Constitution.[23]

The Constitution not only transformed the sovereign Colonies into a unified national government, but also gave them definite military powers. Congress now could "declare war, commission privateers, raise and support armies, build and maintain a navy, and approve all regulations necessary to govern the Armed Forces."[24] In addition, the Constitution transferred much of the states' authority over the militia to Congress, somewhat fearing that an incident like Shay's Rebellion could disrupt the country again. It also created the Office of the President, endowing that position with powers as Commander-in-Chief of the Army, Navy, and the militia, when called to active service for the nation.[25]

With George Washington as President and the Federalists in control of the government, the Nation began its new course in the late 1700s. Almost immediately, they had to contend with a variety of foreign relations problems and domestic issues, most notably how to deal with the Indians on the frontier. The majority of Indian tribes arrayed against the United States in the Northwest Territory stretched from western New York well into central Ohio. With the British as their ally, they held many of the strategic posts along the Ohio River and the Great Lakes region.

---

[22] Shay's rebellion was a popular unrest that occurred in the fall of 1786 in western Massachusetts (See Urwin, 36).
[23] Urwin, 35-36.
[24] Ibid., 39.

Washington's government had espoused avoiding war and negotiating peace treaties with the Indians, realizing that they could purchase the land they desired at less expense than the blood it would cost to win it. Throughout the 1790s, the Federalists responded to every crisis with the Indians, however, with military power, and used defense requirements in the west to demand a large regular army.[26] In 1794, the government applied military force—the newly created Legion—to defeat the Indians in the Northwest Territory and to destroy the British influence over the Indians. That same year, the administration mobilized 15,000 militiamen to crush the Whiskey Rebellion in Western Pennsylvania.[27]

In the years to follow, defense of the homeland took on definite structure as the American army "developed into a functioning organization with defined missions, ordered internal life, and clearly outlined structure."[28] The Quasi-war with France in 1798 and 1799 brought about a dedicated navy and coastal defense system. In the early 1800s, however, America adopted a passive defense policy which was quickly tested, both domestically and internationally.

In 1812 the United States declared war against Britain in response to continued violations of American neutrality at sea during her war with Napoleonic France. At the same time, internal homeland defense issues plagued the country from a regional perspective. Americans were contending with British intervention from Canada, and naval raids along the coastal states. Likewise, they were threatened by the Creek Indians in the Southwest, and the Indian Confederacy under Shawnee Chief Tecumseh in the Northwest, who posed possibly the greatest threat to American security.[29] To deal with these threats to the American homeland, the United States enacted legislation to increase the size of its Army and the militia. It also commissioned

---

[25] Wright and MacGregor, 216-217.

[26] Kohn, 91-95.

[27] Ibid., 139. The Whiskey Rebellion erupted in Pittsburgh, PA in July 1794 as a protest against an excise tax on whiskey. Though citizens in other states, such as Maryland, Kentucky, Georgia, and the Carolinas, shared the same discontent, Rebels from Pennsylvania acted out on their outrage by attacking whiskey tax collector John Neville's estate. With the Legion committed against the Indians, the government had to rely on the militia to suppress the insurrection (See Millet and Maslowski, 98).

[28] Ibid., 188-189.

[29] Millet and Maslowski, 107.

privateers to help break British blockades on the coast. Claiming victory against both external and internal foes, the U.S. completed the next century with domestic development and territorial expansion as a priority. The government resumed their passive defense policy, keeping a small professional Army with the militia to augment internal defense, and a small professional Navy and coastal fortification system to protect shipping and defend against external threats.[30]

The Armed Forces as Posse Comitatus

America's Armed Forces played pivotal roles in the country's expansion, its economic development, and in maintaining domestic tranquility. In the later 1800s, for example, the Army "explored wilderness, built transportation networks, guarded settlers, and fought wars against Indians" all in the name of "Manifest Destiny."[31] The 1800s were also a period that saw the maturation of American policy toward domestic disorders, namely, use of military forces in domestic emergencies. Beginning with the presidency of Thomas Jefferson, the government embraced a broader policy toward use of Armed Forces to back federal law. The use of regulars and militia became commonplace in domestic disorders such as quelling rebellions and local uprisings, enforcing national embargos, intervening in election riots, and suppressing slave revolts. The 1850s, in particular, with the expansion of American territory at the end of the Mexican War, marked the first legal use of the Army as a *posse comitatus*.[32] In this regard, military forces were used to establish and maintain federal supremacy in the new territories, but more often in regards to the spread of slavery.[33]

---

[30] Ibid., 119.

[31] Ibid., 123.

[32] In accordance with the opinion delivered by Attorney General Caleb Cushing which later was called the "Cushing Doctrine," U.S. Marshals and local sheriffs could call on any and all organized bodies of state militia as well as officers, soldiers, sailors and marines in federal units in their districts into service to help maintain the peace, and in the enforcement of federal law. Cushing's opinions became legal doctrines in name only until after the Civil War (See Coakley, 132).

[33] Robert W. Coakley, *The Role of Federal Military Forces in Domestic Disorders, 1789-1878* (Washington, DC: U.S. Government Printing Office, 1988), 69, 92, 106, 128.

During no period in American history did the Army play a more significant role in civil government than during the era of Reconstruction. Between 1865 and 1877, the Army served as police and performed judicial functions. They oversaw local governments—actually, under military rule, commanders of the Army's military districts were the local government—and continued to deal with domestic disturbances with focused attention on the ex-Confederate States in the South.[34] The passing of the Civil Rights Act in April 1866 specifically committed both land and naval forces to serve as *posse comitatus* in service to federal Marshals to prohibit racial discrimination. The passing of the First Reconstruction Act in 1867, which declared military rule in the South, officially allowed military commanders to employ troops without request from civil authorities to suppress disturbances and to enforce federal laws. With the emergence of guerilla activity in the South and the rise of secret organizations like the Ku Klux Klan, who promoted white supremacy, the national government under President Grant continued to lift legal restrictions against the use of military force in execution of civil law.

Along with these measures, in the 1870s, Congress passed two Enforcement Acts that imposed the Fifteenth Amendment, allowing blacks to vote. Like other Acts passed during Reconstruction, it allowed federal marshals to use portions of land and naval forces or the militia, as necessary, to serve as a *posse comitatus* of the local county to deal with violations of the law. Additionally, the Acts allowed the President to employ military units under military command to intervene in such cases, and authorized Army troops to serve as police for federal elections.[35]

After the election of 1876, the stationing of the Army at polling places and political events provoked a reaction from Congress, as Democrats accused federal troops of intimidating voters and allowing voter fraud instead of ensuring national defense. The 45th Congress, with a Democratic majority, passed the *Posse Comitatus* Act as part of the Army Appropriations Act of June 18, 1878 in response to frequent use of troops in civil law enforcement in the South during

---

[34] Ibid., 268.
[35] Ibid., 288, 299, 308.

Reconstruction.[36] The Act accordingly reinstated regular civil authority in the South and

confined the role of the military to that which had been viewed to be appropriate before the Civil

War.[37] The Act stated:

> From and after the passage of this act it shall not be lawful to employ
> any part of the Army of the United States as a posse comitatus, or
> otherwise, for the purpose of executing the laws, except in such cases
> and under such circumstances as such employment of said force may be
> expressly authorized by the Constitution or by act of Congress; and no
> money appropriated by this act shall be used to pay any of the expenses
> incurred in the employment of any troops in violation of this section
> and any person willfully violating the provisions of this section shall be
> deemed guilty of a misdemeanor, and on conviction thereof shall be
> punished a fine not exceeding ten thousand dollars or imprisonment not
> exceeding two years, or by both such fine and imprisonment.[38]

In the succeeding years since the passage of the *Posse Comitatus* Act, the employment of

the Armed Forces for domestic defense issues continued to be widespread, however for more

mundane purposes. The Army helped maintain civil order as the West continued to develop,

served as stabilizers of social and political unrest brought about by the industrial revolution, and

protected the lives and rights of racial minorities throughout the country. The Army remained the

first option for internal defense crises, although that domestic role over the years was

progressively reduced, as the government began to pay more attention to constitutional and legal

processes.[39]

The Problem of Posse Comitatus Today

In legal terms, the *Posse Comitatus* Act is a criminal statute, yet, while it provides for

conviction of any one who uses servicemen to enforce civil law, no one to this day has ever been

---

[36] Craig T. Trebilcock, "The Myth of Posse Comitatus," *Journal of Homeland Defense*, October 27, 2000, [journal on-line]; available from at http://www.homelanddefense.org; Internet; accessed October 2001.

[37] Paul Schott Stevens, *U.S. Armed Forces and Homeland Defense: The Legal Framework*, (Washington, D.C.: Center for Strategic and International Studies, 2001), 23.

[38] Coakley, 344.

[38] Ibid.

[39] Clayton D. Laurie and Ronald H. Cole, *The Role of Federal Military Forces in Domestic Disorders 1877-1945*, (Washington, DC: U.S. Government Printing Office, 1997), vii.

prosecuted for violation of the Act.[40] Many attribute this gross lack of convictions in 124 years of

existence of the statute to the numerous legal loopholes "by exception" resident in the Act.[41] In

the same way, others contend that its erosion over the years has circumvented its usefulness.[42]

Still another view expresses the opinion that though *Posse Comitatus* has limited application, the

policies underlying the Act are of great significance. In this manner, the legislation passed since

the 1980s, for example, offer a broad range of lawful activities for civil authorities to employ use

of the military in the domestic environment, apart from the exercise of police powers, including

activities in support of law enforcement.[43] There is also the somewhat unpopular view that

military involvement in domestic affairs is here to stay, and that immediate changes to the *Posse*

Comitatus Act are necessary to fulfill the goals of U.S. National Security Strategy.[44]

Why the confusion and abundance of interpretations over such a dated piece of

legislation? If the *Posse Comitatus* Act is relevant, why have lawmakers circumvented its use for

the past twenty-two years? And if the Act is eroding, why keep it? Why not either change the

Act to reflect the current strategic and domestic environment, or rescind the statute all together?

As evident above, one major problem with the *Posse Comitatus* Act is that there are too

many different interpretations of its application. In fact, at the center of any discussion about

Posse Comitatus is the enduring debate of how and when (and if) the government should employ

regular military forces and other DOD assets for domestic emergencies or terrorist attacks in

support of U.S. national defense. This debate aside, one point is clear: an apparent disconnect

now exists between the domestic environment in the America of the late eighteenth century when

---

[40] Benson, 3.

[41] "Exception" refers to the wording of the original appropriations bill, Chapter 263, Section 15, as approved on June 18, 1878: ..."except in such cases and under such circumstances as such employment of said force may be expressly authorized by the Constitution or by act of Congress..."

[42] Trebilcock, 2. Erosion in this case refers to repeated circumvention by subsequent legislation. Tribelcock writes that, "since 1980, the Congress and the President have significantly eroded the prohibitions of the Act in order to meet a variety of law enforcement challenges" such as the War of Drugs.

[43] Stevens, 27.

[44] Steven L. Miller, *The Military, Domestic Law Enforcement, and Posse Comitatus: A Time for Change*, (Maxwell Air Force Base, AL: Air Command and Staff College), v.

the Nation implemented *Posse Comitatus* (with a heavy reliance on militia forces and local juries for law enforcement) and the environment within the United States today.

One recent study illustrates this disconnect by highlighting the fact that during the Constitutional debates of the late eighteenth century, the threat of a standing national army to local cultural independence seemed to have been naturally associated with the idea of police powers. North Americans associated police powers with the imposition of force to both regulate violence, and to change social norms. Thus, today, the great distance between local police forces and the U.S. Army is a historical result of the conceptual intimacy that fatally existed between the military and police power in eighteenth century North America.[45] The dilemma that this statement lends to the issue of *Posse Comitatus* is namely that the current environment is such that local police powers (and federal agencies, e.g. DOJ and FBI) are now incapable of exclusively managing the threat nor are they solely capable of responding to the consequences of violent acts to the U.S. homeland. The national military, on the other hand, maintains many of the tools and skills required to both assist and perhaps serve as lead agency, but is technically prohibited by law from providing the full measure of assistance, barring presidential declaration of national emergency.

Another viewpoint of this study postulates that during the conception of the U.S. Constitution, the power of the federal government was habitually associated with the threat of tyranny within the same axiom that associated military power with tyranny. As North American political culture has evolved, the fear of tyranny from a central government has faded somewhat, but the same axiom of military tyranny remains.[46] Very simply, perhaps many in America still fear direct military involvement in domestic affairs.

A greater problem with the *Posse Comitatus* Act comes as a result of the September 11, 2001, terrorist attacks. The recent attacks have given new emphasis in American policy from

---

[45] Geoffrey Demarest, "The Overlap of Military and Police in Latin America," *Foreign Military Studies Office Publications* (April, 1995), 3.

force projection to defense of the Nation as the foundation of strategy. As stated in the 2001 Quadrennial Defense Review, "…the defense strategy restores the emphasis once placed on defending the United States and its land, sea, air, and space approaches. It is essential to safeguard the Nation's way of life, its political institutions, and the source of its capacity to project decisive military power overseas."[47] Indeed, as the Nation scrambles to develop its action plan to address shortfalls in deterrence and prevention of attacks on the U.S. homeland, any existing legislation prohibitive of the government taking necessary measures to ensure defense of the homeland is possibly all but void. Attorney General John Ashcroft adamantly argued a similar point regarding new homeland investigative powers for the FBI and CIA on Capital Hill immediately after September 11, 2001, stating that, "Technology has dramatically outpaced our statutes… The American people do not have the luxury of unlimited time in erecting the necessary defenses to future acts. Terrorism is a clear and present danger to Americans today."[48]

Lastly, whereas American homeland security policy has historically been defensive and reactive, policy must now shift to a more offensive and proactive focus, to prevent or deter actions against U.S. interests at home and around the world. This proactive focus must be inclusive of a campaign that incorporates: an information campaign that maintains American confidence in government, as well as builds a coalition dedicated on eradicating global terror; a robust integrated intelligence capability that fuses information from law enforcement, regulatory, financial, national and military sources into actionable intelligence; a multi-dimensional direct action capability of military and non-military formations which can combine all the powers of the Nation fully against U.S. enemies; and a rapid response capability beyond consequence management, that enables the Nation to respond quickly to mitigate the effects of any attack. Homeland Security is perhaps the most difficult and important mission the U.S. (military) will

---

[46] Ibid.

[47] Department of Defense, *Quadrennial Defense Review Report* (Washington, D.C., Government Printing Office, 2001), 14.

[48] Quoted testimonial of Attorney General John Ashcroft, Source unknown.

undertake since World War II. As such, it must be combined arms, joint, interagency, coalition

and multi-dimensional in nature.[49] With the minor exception of legislation to enhance America's

War on Drugs, the *Posse Comitatus* Act remains a block against military involvement with

federal agencies in such a flexible endeavor.

---

[49] William J. Miller, Sven Erichsen, and Jeffery K. Toomer, *Homeland Security: A Campaign Framework*, (Concept paper, Command and General Staff College-School of Advanced Military Studies, 2001), 1.

CHAPTER THREE

U.S. MODEL FOR HOMELAND DEFENSE AND THE INADEQUACIES OF POSSE COMITATUS

In order to illustrate the inadequacies of the *Posse Comitatus* Act and how the Act

hinders the development of effective homeland defense doctrine today, it is necessary to explore

the broader context in which U.S. homeland security programs are developed. This chapter

discusses the framework for U.S. homeland security doctrine. Additionally, it will explore the

growing irrelevance of the *Posse Comitatus* Act by focusing on changes to the Act brought on by

growth of the military involvement in the War on Drugs in the 1980s, and expanding use of

military forces in other domestic support operations.

The U.S. Model

The justifications for homeland security activities in the U.S. are embedded in

Constitutional, legal, strategic, domestic and political contexts. The Preamble of the Constitution

sets the immediate framework for defense of the homeland by declaring its purpose as "to form a

more perfect Union, establish justice, insure domestic tranquility, provide for the common

defense, promote the general welfare, and secure the blessings of liberty to ourselves and our

posterity." Article I, Section 8, provides the authorization for employment of military forces

domestically by stating, "The Congress shall have power to…raise and support Armies; to

provide and maintain a Navy; and…to provide for calling forth the militia to execute the laws of

the Union, suppress insurrections and repel invasions." Article IV, Section 4 expands this

authority by pledging, "to protect each (State in the Union) against invasion."[50]

The current (2000) version of the U.S. National Security Strategy (NSS) provides the

strategic context for homeland security tasks. Entitled *A National Security Strategy for a Global*

---

[50] "Constitution of the United States, September 17, 1787" in Wright and MacGregor, 214-219.

Age, the NSS identifies acts of terrorism and weapons of mass destruction as two of the nations special concerns.

> We also must identify and address new national security challenges, accentuated by new technology and open borders. We have identified a new security agenda that addresses contemporary threats such as the proliferation of nuclear, chemical and biological weapons, terrorism, and international crime. New efforts must continue to build on initiatives such as the extension of the Nonproliferation Treaty, the containment of nations seeking to acquire and use weapons of mass destruction, increased antiterrorism cooperation, stepped up efforts to combat trafficking in drugs, arms, and human-beings, and our first-ever national strategy for cybersecurity.[51]

The NSS conclusively states that the nation must have effective capabilities to counter these threats, and that the solution is more in the realm of an interagency effort, requiring the cooperation and participation of every level of government as well as the private sector.

To compliment the NSS, the most recent version of the National Military Strategy (NMS), published in 1997, upholds defense of the homeland as the singular effort that enables successful execution of other portions of U.S. defense strategy. It states, "Our National Military Strategy depends first and foremost upon the United States remaining secure from external threats. A secure homeland is fundamental to U.S. global leadership."[52] A later published planning document specific to the Army lists ensuring sovereignty of the U.S. as a vital interest. The document, the 1999 *Army Strategic Planning Guidance* (ASPG), revises mission areas for the Army to include support to homeland security. As executive agent for the DOD Domestic Preparedness Program, the ASPG states that, "the Army will provide capabilities to conduct operations to support homeland defense. America's Army must be ready to defend U.S. territory,

---

[51] The White House, *A National Security Strategy for a Global Age* (Washington, D.C., Government Printing Office, 2000), iii.

[52] Department of Defense, *National Military Strategy: Shape, Respond, Prepare Now, A Military Strategy for a New Era* [on-line], available from http://www.dtic.mil/jcs/core/nms.html, Internet, accessed 27 March 2002.

population, and infrastructure against strategic attack and against emerging transnational threats."[53]

In domestic and political contexts, the Clinton Administration declared a national emergency in November 1994 because of growing concerns about proliferation of WMD. The Executive Order declared WMD and its delivery means an "unusual and extraordinary threat to the national security, foreign policy, and economy of the U.S."[54] The Administration provided subsequent policy guidance for combating terrorism and WMD in two Presidential Decision Directives (PDD). PDD 39, "U.S. Policy Towards Counter-Terrorism," was published in June 1995 and provided direction for combating and reducing vulnerabilities to terrorism, deterring and responding to terrorist acts, and preventing and managing the consequences of WMD use. The policy delineated agency responsibilities for dealing with WMD by terrorists in the categories of crisis response and consequence management.[55] Domestically, the PDD assigned lead agency responsibility to the Department of Justice, with the FBI responsible for crisis response activities and FEMA responsible for consequence management.[56] PDD 62, "Protecting Against Unconventional Threats to the Homeland and Americans Overseas," in May 1998 established the Office of the National Coordinator for Security, Infrastructure Protection and Counter-Terrorism as overseer of the Nation's efforts to combat terrorism.[57]

In addition to these two policy measures, Congressional legislation has also helped formulate current U.S. homeland security policy. In response to the June 1996 bombing of the Al Khobar barracks in Saudi Arabia where nineteen Americans died, the Senate adopted the Nunn-Lugar-Domenici Amendment. Subsequent to this amendment, Congress passed the National

---

[53] U.S. Army, *Army Strategic Planning Guidance* (Washington, D.C., Government Printing Office, 1999), ii and 52.

[54] Larsen and Peters, 11.

[55] Crisis response is those activities conducted prior to and hopefully preventing the use of weapons of mass destruction by terrorists. Consequence management deals with mitigating and alleviating the effects of a chemical or biological attack, including preparatory work (See "Domestic Preparedness" [on-line] available from http://www.fas.org/spp/starwars/program/domestic.htm); Internet; accessed 25 February 2002.

[56] The White House, *PDD-39*.

Defense Authorization Act of 1997. Together, these two pieces of legislation focused on preventing terrorist assaults with WMD in the U.S., helping U.S. cities and states handle the consequences of such attacks, and authorized increased funding for national counter-terrorism efforts. Specific to DOD, the Act directed DOD to create a training program at the federal, state and local level regarding response to use of or threats of WMD. The Act specified use of the National Guard to carry out this program, and directed the development of domestic terrorism rapid response teams from the Armed Forces capable of aiding government officials at all levels in the detection, neutralization, containment, dismantlement, and disposal of WMD.[58]

Amazingly, despite such recent and significant policy guidance to advance homeland security readiness, the U.S. government still falls short in terms of having a cohesive, coordinated doctrine for defense of the homeland. Before September 11, 2001, critics argued that U.S. resources to prevent or respond to domestic emergencies, such as terrorist attacks with WMD, were distributed amongst several different agencies, at different levels of government, and with little to no coordination between them. These organizations totaled sixty-one agencies at the federal level alone.[59] Given the nature of the new non-conventional threat environment—to include terrorism, proliferation of WMD, attacks on U.S. critical infrastructure, the international drug trade, organized crime, and a host of transnational threats—the mission is immense, and no single federal agency or department could possibly address all the Nation's security requirements alone.

After September 11, the Bush Administration's establishment of the Office of Homeland Security, with a charge to provide a coordinated and comprehensive national strategy to help protect the United States against terrorist threats or attacks is a solid beginning. "The President's Executive Order establishe[d] the Office of Homeland Defense and the Homeland Security Council to develop and coordinate a comprehensive national strategy to strengthen protections

---

[57] The White House, *PDD-62.*
[58] Larsen and Peters, 12-15.

against terrorist threats or attacks in the United States. The new team coordinates federal, state, and local counter-terrorism efforts.[60]

Also most recently, DOD published the 2001 Quadrennial Defense Review (QDR) Report that restores America's defense focus internally to enable her to be effective abroad. To that end, the QDR lists defending the Nation from attack as the foundation of its defense strategy, and defending the Nation from all enemies as the highest priority of the U.S. military.

> Defending the Nation from attack is the foundation of strategy. As the tragic September terror attacks demonstrate, potential adversaries will seek to threaten the centers of gravity of the United States, its allies, and its friends. As the U.S. military increased its ability to project power at long-range, adversaries have noted the relative vulnerability of the U.S. homeland... Therefore, the defense strategy restores the emphasis once placed on defending the United States and its land, sea, air, and space approaches. It is essential to safeguard the Nation's way of life, its political institutions, and the source of its capacity to project decisive military power overseas.
>
> The highest priority of the U.S. military is to defend the Nation from all enemies. The United States will maintain sufficient military forces to protect the U.S. domestic population, its territory, and its critical defense-related infrastructure against attacks emanating from outside U.S. borders, as appropriate under U.S. law... [T]he U.S. military will be prepared to respond in a decisive manner to acts of international terrorism committed on U.S. territory or the territory of an ally.[61]

Even with the creation of the Office of Homeland Security, and the grandiose words of the 2001 QDR, there is no simple organizational solution. To name just two key areas of tension among many, homeland defense still raises issues of the role of government in society, and the long-standing issue of citizens' rights.[62] DOD's role in homeland security is still tenuous, and the Department treats it carefully. In the 2001 QDR, for example, DOD continues to downplay any significant first response responsibilities for national emergencies. DOD also firmly rejects any role as sole or lead agency for homeland security activities.

---

[59] Howard, 115 and 122.

[60] The White House, "What is the Office of Homeland Security?" [on-line]; available from http://www.whitehouse.gov/response/faq-homeland.html; Internet; accessed 25 February 2002.

[61] DOD, *Quadrennial Defense Review Report*, iii, 14 and 18.

[62] Terrence Kelly, "An Organizational Framework for Homeland Defense," *Parameters* (Autumn 2001):

To add to the dilemma, while the trend in the 1980s and 1990s has featured an extensive use of DOD assets for the War on Drugs and a host of domestic consequence management tasks,[63] many still cling to the *Posse Comitatus* Act as a historic "bulwark of our democratic society" which prohibits military involvement in direct law enforcement activities, unless specifically authorized under the Constitution or Act of Congress.[64] This one legal restriction is significant in terms of crafting future homeland defense doctrine in the current operating environment, especially when many consider DOD, and the Army in particular, as the Nation's best resource in the domestic-security arena. Specifically, the Army (and DOD) maintains the best equipment to respond to incidents of WMD; possesses the preponderance of resources to execute a robust, integrated intelligence network; and has the inherent capabilities of providing a true interagency command and control architecture for a consolidated national homeland security effort. Arguably, the current operating environment that the U.S. now faces may not allow ample time for an act of Congress or Presidential declaration of emergency to provide the safety and protection that Americans expect, nor to prevent and deter acts of terror from ever happening in the first place. What good is the world's best military if you cannot use it for the country's number one defense priority, anyway?[65]

Historical Application of the Act

The *Posse Comitatus* Act, as originally passed in 1878, was directed singularly towards the Army to prevent it from enforcing domestic law as stated first in an appropriations bill,

---

05-16.

[63] PDD 39 and a host of assorted legislation permit DOD to develop and maintain plans and capabilities to respond to threats or acts of terrorism, including WMD. DOD has published several directives establishing policy and assigning responsibility for providing military assistance to civil authorities including specific policy for assistance to civil law enforcement officials in emergencies involving terrorism and WMD (See Jeffrey D. Brake, *Terrorism and the Military's Role in Domestic Crisis Management: Background and Issues for Congress*, April 19, 2001 [on-line]; available from http://www.fas.org/irp/crs/rl30928.pdf; Internet; accessed 25 February 2002.

[64] Thomas R. Lujan, "Legal Aspects of Domestic Employment of the Army," *Parameters* (Autumn 1997): 83.

[65] Aaron Weiss, "When Terror Strikes, Who Should Respond?" *Parameters* (Autumn 2001): 4. This question is the derivative of a sub-title in Weiss's article.

Chapter 263, Section 15, and subsequently in Title 18 United States Code (USC), Part I, Chapter 6, Section 1385. The Act was extended to the Air Force under the National Security Act of 1947, which created the Department of Defense.[66] In accordance with DOD Directive 5525.5, *Restrictions on Participation of DOD Personnel in Civilian Actions* (January 15, 1986), the limitations of the *Posse Comitatus* Act administratively apply to the Navy and Marine Corps as well.[67] The Act does not apply to the Coast Guard.[68] Neither does it apply to the National Guard, unless federalized by the President under Title 10, USC.[69]

In simple terms, the *Posse Comitatus* Act prohibits direct involvement of military personnel in enforcing civilian laws, as stated in the existing Title 10 reference to *Posse Comitatus*:

> Sec. 375. Restrictions on Participation of DOD Personnel in Civilian Actions. The Secretary of Defense shall prescribe such regulation as may be necessary to ensure that any activity (including the provision of any equipment of facility or the assignment or detail of any personnel) under this chapter *does not include or permit direct participation* by a member of the Army, Navy, Air Force, or Marine Corps in a search, seizure, arrest, or other similar activity unless participation in such activity by such member is otherwise authorized by law.[70]

Direct involvement (participation) thus connotes performing typical police functions. In an attempt to therefore define permissible actions that military personnel can provide in support to civilian authorities (and law enforcement), the federal courts have commonly applied an "active" or "passive" test. Active participation in law enforcement, such as making arrests, is considered a violation of the *Posse Comitatus* Act; passive support, such as providing equipment, training, use of facilities, or even the sharing of some kinds of intelligence, is not a violation.[71]

---

[66] Bonnie Baker, "The Origins of the Posse Comitatus,"[on-line]; available from http://www.airpower maxwell.af.mil/airchronicles/cc/baker1/html; Internet; accessed 23 October 2001.
[67] Trebilcock, 5 (endnotes).
[68] 14 U.S.C. Section 1 (1997).
[69] Trebilcock, 1-2.
[70] 14 U.S.C. Section 1 (1997).
[71] Trebilcock, 2.

Weakening of the Act

Changes to the Act

Throughout the last century, there have been several suspensions of the *Posse Comitatus* Act in order to allow the use of military forces for law enforcement functions. These include the employment of federal troops in Chicago in 1919 to end rioting; use of the Armed Forces in Washington, D.C. in 1932 against Bonus Marchers; and during the Truman administration, use of troops to end a workers' strike after the railroads had become nationalized.[72] The War on Drugs and the subsequent 1982 DOD Defense Authorization Act, however, is considered by several as the period when the most substantive changes and thus the weakening of the *Posse Comitatus* Act has occurred.

In the legislation of the 1982 Defense Authorization Act several amendments (Sections 371-382) provide for increased use of DOD assets or direct DOD involvement in assisting civil law enforcement. The Act allowed military authorities to share information relative to violations of the law with law enforcement personnel; allowed DOD to loan equipment, associated supplies and parts, and training facilities; permitted DOD to train civilian law enforcement; allowed DOD to support civil authorities by maintaining and operating equipment, with stated limits; provided for the monitoring of suspects both outside of and up to twenty-five miles inside the U.S. borders; and authorized the military to detain civilians in order to turn them over to appropriate law enforcement personnel. Despite these increased provisions, however, the Act still prohibited military personnel from directly participating in searches, seizures, arrests or other similar activities.[73] Consequent to the 1982 Defense Authorization Act, DOD and DOJ, in 1985, signed one additional memorandum permitting military criminal investigative organizations to investigate civilians suspected of drug crimes on military installations or involved with military

---

[72] Baker, 2.
[73] Nolon J. Benson, Jr., *The Posse Comitatus Act: Is There a Need for Change?* (Carlisle Barracks, PA: U.S. Army War College, 1998), 8.

members. In 1988, 1996, and 1997 still more legislation specified relationships between military and civilian agencies during chemical emergencies, to include tasking DOD as executive agent for a program aimed at training local first responders in responding to WMD.[74]

Military Involvement in the War on Drugs

Clearly, America's War on Drugs has necessitated a higher level of cooperation and seamless integration of several systems between the military and drug-law enforcers. In fact, military participation in the anti-drug effort is perhaps one of the best indicators not only of the erosion of the *Posse Comitatus* Act, but also of the future role of military involvement in domestic security affairs.

Every President since Richard Nixon has included the fight against drugs as a key component of their domestic strategy. The Reagan administration was perhaps the first to apply earnest efforts to interdict the flow of illegal drugs into the U.S. For this effort, active duty Navy seaman and Air Force pilots, as well as activated Air National Guard forces were routinely employed to work alongside civilian drug enforcers to patrol the Caribbean, Gulf of Mexico and associated coastlines for drug traffickers. President Bush, in 1989, was the first to appoint a "drug czar." With that, Congress identified DOD as lead agency for anti-drug intelligence and increased the DOD anti-drug budget to $438 million. The boldest and most significant move towards military involvement in the drug war has been the creation of Joint Task Force (JTF)-6.[75] Established in 1989, JTF-6 is headquarted just outside of Fort Bliss, Texas, and its mission is to coordinate joint military and civilian law enforcement anti-drug operations along the U.S-Mexico border. The command today boasts over 700 soldiers and conducts nearly 550 law enforcement support missions annually.[76] Under the operational control of Joint Forces Command, JTF-6 essentially processes requests from law enforcement agencies for military support. These

---

[74] Steven L. Miller, *The Military, Domestic Law Enforcement, and Posse Comitatus: A Time for Change*, (Maxwell Air Force Base, AL: Air Command and Staff College), 8.
[75] Miller, 11-12.

requests are validated to contain an appropriate drug nexus, and subsequently approved by deployment orders by the Joint Chiefs of Staff. Missions normally include area surveillance and reporting, to include ferrying law enforcement officers via aviation assets. Active duty and National Guard soldiers, to include Special Forces detachments, are typically attached to JTF-6 from their parent units for six-month periods.[77]

One other measure towards the furtherance of U.S. military involvement was the appointment of retired General Barry McCaffrey, the former Commander-in-Chief of Southern Command, as "drug czar" or Director of the Office of National Drug Control Policy. General McCaffrey was influential in shifting the Clinton administration's focus of the national drug effort from an interdiction-in-transit role, to one of strengthening the U.S. borders and providing assistance to source countries to combat the production of illegal drugs.[78] McCaffrey was also able to increase the intelligence effort aimed at uncovering production and transportation pipelines. The interesting consequence of this effort has been the increased detection of large numbers of illegal immigrants attempting to enter the U.S.[79] McCaffrey resolutely contends that, if unchecked, America's drug problems can only grow worse, leading to thousands of American deaths and excessive costs to the U.S. society over the coming years.

> The military is the best option for no other reason than the military possesses the training, equipment, advanced technology, and command and control structure that surpasses any civilian law enforcement agency. Whether its AWACS support or the latest generation of hand-held thermal imager, the military is infinitely better equipped to provide detection, surveillance, reconnaissance, and targeting capabilities than other state or federal agencies. The military is typically on the cutting edge of emerging technologies and these technologies can oftentimes be easily adapted to the drug war environment.[80]

If statistics prove anything, then the statistics of U.S. military involvement in the drug crisis prove that the military is in for the long haul. DOD has received a consistently increasing

---

[76] Ibid.

[77] Thomas R. Lujan, "Legal Aspects of Domestic Employment of the Army," *Parameters* (Autumn, 1997): 4.

[78] Examples of this include U.S. aid to the Columbian and Mexican governments.

[79] Ibid., 12.

anti-drug budget and has commensurately involved more military personnel in the drug war. One writer reports that the National Guard alone has more personnel on counter-narcotics missions (as part of JTF-6) than the Drug Enforcement Agency has special agents on duty.[81] The rationale for such action should not be as surprising as some make it out to be, however. Both the National Security Strategy and the National Military Strategy include drug trafficking under the umbrella of threats to U.S. interests, values, and its citizens.[82] Like terrorism, the National Military Strategy identifies the illegal drug trade as an asymmetric challenge and transnational danger which warrants the unique military capabilities that support to domestic authorities can provide, combating direct threats to the U.S. homeland.[83]

Military Involvement in Domestic Support Operations

The War on Drugs is not the only effort taken on by civilian law enforcement where military participation and intervention has been needed and where conflicts with the *Posse Comitatus* Act have arisen and in most cases, been circumvented. More recent examples of domestic employment of the military reveal several points of contention. In August 1992, the U.S. responded to the devastating effects of Hurricane Andrew in southern Florida by deploying one brigade each from both the 82nd Airborne Division and the 10th Mountain Division to provide disaster relief. Disaster assistance is authorized under the Robert T. Stafford Disaster Relief Act of 1984, is applicable only within the U.S. and its territories, requires a state governor to request a presidential declaration of emergency for the state following a disaster, and allows the employment of active duty soldiers to respond to crises under the direction of FEMA.[84] During the Hurricane Andrew relief operation, two specific *Posse Comitatus* conflicts occurred. First,

---

[80] Ibid., 13.
[81] "Drug War Facts: Military Participation in the Drug War, 1997", [on-line]; available from http://www.csdp.org/factbook/military.htm; Internet; accessed 11 March 2002.
[82] The White House, A *National Security Strategy for a Global Age,* 18; and Chairman of the Joint Chiefs, *National Military Strategy of the United States of America,* 9.
[83] Chairman of the Joint Chiefs, *National Military Strategy of the United States of America,* 17.
[84] Lujan, 1.

authorities had to replace active duty soldiers with Guardsmen to provide security at aid stations and storage facilities so that the potential for active soldiers to have to make citizen's arrests of illegal immigrants would not occur. Second, a group of soldiers was found bivouacking too close to an election site. The soldiers were clearly in violation of the *Posse Comitatus* Act, however, a DOJ review deemed their presence and specific mission justified and did not require them to move.[85]

The "not guilty" verdict of the Rodney King trail and resultant rioting and devastation that occurred in Los Angeles in April 1992 provoked a presidential order authorizing the deployment of federal troops to quell the domestic violence. The statutory authority allowing the President to utilize federal troops for national emergencies automatically exempts federal troops from the prohibitions of the *Posse Comitatus* Act. In Los Angeles, there were widespread misunderstandings of the proper role of active-duty forces and federalized National Guard units in the emergency situation. The JTF commander believed his unit was constrained by the Act, and therefore assumed they could not participate in law enforcement activities. The commander's misplaced assertions about *Posse Comitatus* led him to refuse law enforcement support missions. Surprisingly, the National Guard units, once federalized, followed the same mistaken patterns. The confusion over *Posse Comitatus* restrictions also hindered distribution of hardware such as night vision goggles, radios, and use of helicopters, which naturally caused a lot of friction between active duty, National Guardsmen, and law enforcement officials.[86] These misunderstandings permeated all military activity throughout the operation, caused the forces on the ground to follow the wrong rules of engagement, and therefore greatly hindered the explicit use of force to quell the violence.[87]

Beyond Domestic Support

---

[85] Ibid., 2.
[86] Baker, 4.
[87] Lujan, 7.

A more recent and no less vivid example of transformation or modification of the *Posse Comitatus* Act is evident in the increasingly common use of Armed Forces as security personnel for national sporting and entertaining events. During the 1996 Summer Olympics in Atlanta over ten thousand soldiers were employed under the guise of deterring terrorism.[88] Considering the uni-bomber incident that occurred during those games, their use was probably justified by most, but behind the scenes soldiers were used for far more activity than security purposes, namely in the transportation arena.

The recent 2001 Winter Olympic Games at Salt Lake City were no different, with the exception being that military presence was mandated by the federal government, to include visits to check on security preparations by both the U.S. Attorney General and the newly appointed Director of the Office of Homeland Security. The same can be said for the World Series, the Superbowl, and most recently, the Grammys. At each event, U.S. military, active and National Guard (federalized), have been on the scene, to provide security, and to deter terrorism. The amazing issue with this is that after September 11, few people are raising any serious questions about the specific use of troops as law enforcement, directly in violation of the *Posse Comitatus* Act.

What Good is the World's Best Military if You Can't Use It?

Critics arguing against using regular military forces in domestic environments have two main points. The first is that employment of active duty military forces in the domestic arena holds the potential for infringement on individual rights.[89] One major tragedy that occurred in the not-to-distant past as part of the War on Drugs is a vivid illustration of this argument. On May 20, 1997, a four-person Marine surveillance team was conducting a counter-drug mission on the Texas-Mexico border, near Redford, Texas, in support of the U.S. Border Patrol. The Marines, trying to remain undetected, happened upon an 18-year-old boy tending his family's goat heard.

---

[88] Trebilcock, 4.

Identifying the boy as having a weapon, and thinking that he had fired upon them, the Marines shot the boy and killed him. Though the Marines were doing what they had been trained to do, the boy's family was awarded a $2 million wrongful death settlement out of court. This incident marked the first U.S. citizen killed by the military on U.S. soil as part of the War on Drugs.[90]

The second argument is that over reliance on the military for domestic protection (i.e. from WMD), may diminish the military's capability to promote U.S. foreign policy and win the nation's wars.[91] It is fact, the U.S. military is busier than it has ever been, and just as the military throughout history has long been used to solve many of the country's complex issues, so today it is being called on more than ever. Since the Gulf War, military forces have embraced the War on Drugs through JTF-6. Along with that, the military has increasingly supported law enforcement in the inner cities. Recent domestic support operations include JTF-LA during the aftermath of the Rodney King trial, and disaster relief missions in Florida following Hurricane Andrew and in Hawaii after Hurricane Iniki. The Navy and Marines participated in disaster relief in the Philippines following the eruption of Mt. Pinatubo in 1992 and again in 1994. Special Forces troops provided advice and equipment to the FBI for their siege and assault of David Koresh's Branch Davidian compound in Waco, Texas in 1994. Today, with the First Lady's emphasis on Armed Forces aiding the nation's failing educational system, the military is engaged in encouraging local children in inner-city schools, with fully developed programs and on-going teaching relationships. The military has also recently assisted environmental clean-ups, promoted wildlife conservation, rebuilt local housing communities, and last but not least, conducted peacekeeping missions in Bosnia and Kosovo. Add to all of these, the on-going war in Afghanistan.[92]

---

[89] Weiss, 1.
[90] Baker, 4 and Benson, 1.
[91] Weiss, 1.
[92] Ibid., 4.

Both of these arguments present valid points that cannot be dismissed. The bottom line of the first case is that the increasing role of Armed Forces in law enforcement (and other areas of domestic concern) does threaten American liberty and therefore breaches a major tenet of the American way of life. The bottom line of the second argument may even be more serious: it has the potential to degrade the military's warfighting capabilities and the abilities of our Armed Forces to protect themselves should they be called upon to go to war.[93]

Each trade-off has drastic consequences. The most drastic consequence, however, would be for the most powerful Nation with the most powerful military in the world to jeopardize its national security at home by *not* employing its Armed Forces—regular or otherwise—in a domestic role to assure the security of its critical infrastructure and its citizenry. This, I argue, would be tragic.

If the world as we know it is different, and U.S. domestic security is at issue, then drastic times call for drastic measures. Moreover, if lawmakers have been using legislation to circumvent the *Posse Comitatus* Act for the past twenty-two years because the Act does not fully satisfy security requirements given the current threat, then it is time for change. Exactly what changes are needed is still debatable. One area that should escape any debate, however, is any legislation that hinders every effort to keep the U.S. homeland secure from external threat. Aside from the current declaration of national emergency, the *Posse Comitatus* Act does not allow for continuous combined arms, joint, interagency, coalition and multi-dimensional operations, which are prerequisites for success in the War on Terror.

---

[93] Ibid., 5.

CHAPTER FOUR

OTHER MODELS FOR HOMELAND DEFENSE

To highlight some possible options for future American homeland defense doctrine in terms of employment of military forces in domestic environments and other response mechanisms, the first three sections of this chapter will examine models of domestic defense for Israel, Canada, and the United Kingdom. The concluding section will summarize the uniqueness of each country's policy and extract those learning points that may be useful in the U.S domestic policy.

The Israeli Model

Few countries in the world have had to maintain more focus on internal security than Israel. The importance that Israel gives its national security stems from the very real threat posed by the country's Arab neighbors. Israelis traditionally view the Arab-Israeli conflict as a continuous war, which lays dormant only between battles or the next incident. Since 1988, the Israelis have also had to contend with sustained protests, violence, and terrorism from Palestinians in the occupied territories. Furthermore, today, with many Middle Eastern countries possessing the means to deliver chemical and biological weapons, the threat to Israel's national security becomes even more acute. National defense for the Israelis has become their number one priority. With such a high priority on defense throughout its entire society, and the vast involvement and influence that the Israeli Defense Force (IDF) has had in the government's defense policies since 1980, some have argued that Israel's supposed democratic form of government has most resembled a praetorian society. Others however support the Israeli defense stance as necessary measures given the constant threats to their security.[94]

---

[94] Department of the Army, *DA Pam 550-25, Israel: A Country Study* (Washington, D.C., Government

In the face of such perceived Arab and Palestinian threats, Israeli policy makers and citizens alike embrace the need for a strong military posture. The IDF was organized with the country's inception in 1948 and charged with the colossal task of guaranteeing their national security. Such a volatile geopolitical situation necessitates extreme measures to ensure Israel's internal defense. Accordingly, since 1992, domestic defense in Israel has come under one of four territorial (or regional) commands called the Home Front Command.[95] This Command "was established with three major responsibilities: to prepare civil defense forces for emergencies; to create a central command for all military and emergency forces; and to serve as the primary military and professional authority for civil defense."[96] Besides its civil defense functions, the Home Front Command is responsible for evacuation of the civilian population, conducts search and rescue operations, maintains and distributes protective kits for populace, and develops passive protection measures.[97]

Unlike in the typical democracy, Israel's Home Front command supersedes civilian authority regarding decisions of domestic security at all times. Though not universally accepted, this policy not only reflects how seriously the Israeli society approaches domestic defense, but also the impact that the IDF and especially the Israeli Army has had in initiation and formulation of government proposals relevant to combating WMD and terrorism.[98] During states of emergency, the Home Front Command has "an unequivocal and unambiguous chain of responsibility, authority and accountability."[99] This greatly facilitates unity of command. Generally, the Homeland Defense Command's authority reaches every civil and military related

---

Printing Office, 1988), 251-252, and 267.

[95] Israeli Defense Forces Official Website, [on-line]; available from http://www.idf.il/english/organization/organization.stm; Internet; accessed 1 March 2002.

[96] Howard, 122.

[97] Israeli Defense Forces, "Homefront Command", [on-line]; available from http://www.idf.il/english/organization/homefront/index.stm; Internet; accessed 1 March 2002.

[98] Noemi Gal-Or, "Countering Terrorism in Israel," in David A. Charters, ed., *The Deadly Sin of Terrorism: Its Effects on Democracy and Civil Liberty in Six Countries* (Westport, CT, Centre for Conflict Studies, University of New Brunswick, 1994), 147.

[99] Howard, 124.

agency, to include medical facilities, which have any part of the nation's preparation for and execution of protective measures in defense of Israel.

Israel prefers a strong offensive security posture over a defensive strategy as the best deterrent to both Arab attacks and other threats to national security. In this regard, Israel embraces a policy of preemptive attacks in the event of overtly hostile acts.[100] Where preemption fails, Israel vows retribution. The preemptive attacks are totally reliant on the ability of the government to provide good intelligence, and at least a reasonable chance of success in the operation.[101] Retribution follows a pattern of semi-proportional response, much like the constant exchange of violence with the Palestinians today.

The other three territorial commands (North, South and Central Regions) are also integral to Israel's domestic defense policy, namely through protection of her borders. In the territories, the army is the governing authority and along with defense of Israel's borders, is also responsible for preventing disturbances of public order and countering terrorism. The territorial commands have three primary internal security tasks: prevention of disturbances and terrorism through public order controls (roadblocks, censorship, and withdrawal of Palestinian privileges for violations); application of emergency regulations in the wake of incidents (curfews, roadblocks, vehicle/building/people searches, or taking punitive measures—detention, deportation, demolition or sealing up of houses); and technically containing/countering terrorism (principle of maximum force).[102]

The Canadian Model

Canada remains America's closest ally and trading partner, and because the two nations share an extensive common border, Canada, by proximity, also shares many of the same

---

[100] DA Pam 550-25, 269. Israel has made it clear to her Arab neighbors that certain actions, even if not overtly hostile or aimed at Israel, would trigger an Israeli preemptive attack. These acts (considered potential causes of war) include: interference with Israeli freedom of navigation in the Strait of Tiran, attempt of an Arab country to acquire WMD, and militarization of the Sinai Peninsula.
[101] Howard, 125.

challenges to domestic security, and in applying military force in domestic emergencies. Canada is governed as a constitutional monarchy under the authority of Queen Elizabeth II of England. Though the Canadian government conducts governmental activity in the Queen's name, Canada operates with total political independence from England. As such, the nature of its government provides an element of flexibility in the conduct of civil-military relations, and in the application of military forces to support civil authority. [103]

Much like the military history of the United States, Canada's national history is replete with incidents of military employment to quell rebellions, disrupt ethnic confrontations, strikes, and prison violence, monitor elections, and to prevent terrorism. [104] Canadian Forces, the national military arm, are primarily organized to protect the nation from external threat, and to promote the government's foreign policy overseas. However, in the past several decades in general, and the last few years in particular, through the execution of a few sensitive domestic operations, Canada has developed a very effective legal and command and control system for interagency coordination, and for employment of Canadian Forces in domestic situations. [105]

Prior to 1988, Canada's domestic operations were governed by their National Defense Act, which limited military assistance to civil authorities to three circumstances: (1) Aid of the Civil Power allowed Providential and Territorial Premiers to request units of the Canadian Forces (regular or reserve) to suppress, prevent, or deal with a riot or disturbance of the peace beyond what the civil authorities could manage; (2) The Civil Defense Order legislation (1952) of the War Measures Act (1914), allowed the Armed Forces to act without specific request from the provinces in the event of nuclear attack to ensure continuity of government and to restore/enforce public order. (Previously, the Act only provided for the flexible employment of the military in the event of war, or invasion, to provide for the peace, security, defense, order and welfare of

---

[102] Gal-Or, 154-156.
[103] Sean M. Maloney, "Domestic Operations, The Canadian Approach," *Parameters* (Autumn, 1997): 136 and 148.
[104] Howard, 129.

Canada.); and (3) Assistance to Civil Authorities including short-term military assistance for operations other than civil disturbance, such as fishery surveillance, counter-narcotics, monitoring pollution, and any help given to local law enforcement shy of troop deployments.[106] One example of Canadian Forces employment for such domestic operations before 1988 included the 1963-70 Front de Liberation du Quebec (FLQ) Crisis, where large troop deployments were employed to suppress the separatist group's seven-year bombing, kidnapping, and assassination campaign in protest of the collapse of the French Canadian provincial establishment in Quebec. Another example is the 1976 Olympic Games in Montreal, where the Canadian government deployed 16,000 military personnel for assistance to civil authority, to serve as a visible deterrent to terrorists.[107]

Since 1988, the Canadians have operated under a reconstructed and somewhat simplified version of its previous laws and policies governing employment of Canadian Forces in domestic crises. The Emergencies Act, for example, replaced the 1914 War Measures Act and specified four types of emergencies: "public welfare (severe natural disasters); public order (threats to the internal security of Canada); international (when intimidation, coercion, or the use of serious force or violence threatens the sovereignty, security, or territorial integrity of Canada; and war (war or other armed conflict, real or imminent, involving Canada or any of its allies).[108]

The Act stipulates the levels of power civil authorities can exert for the different emergencies. "For example, in a Public Order Emergency, the Governor Council is authorized to prohibit public assembly and travel to and from specified areas, and to designate and secure protected places, assume control of public utilities, and impose summary convictions for up to six months of imprisonment.[109] Likewise, this new Act allows Canadian Forces to respond to acts of terrorism through either the Public Order Emergency or an International Emergency.

---

[105]Mahoney, 135.
[106]Ibid., 137.
[107] Ibid., 138-142.
[108] Ibid., 143.

Additionally, the Act specifies that the Canadian government must convene its Parliament within seven days of a declared emergency to provide full rationale for the government's actions. "Any suspension of civil liberties by the government during emergencies is also subject to specific parliamentary oversight."[110]

In 1994, Canada released its Defense White Paper, which provided a review of Canadian defense policy following the fall of the Soviet Union. Along with clarifying roles and missions for Canadian Forces, this new policy defined seven areas in which the authorities could employ military forces for domestic operations. These include: "providing peacetime surveillance and control (sovereignty protection); securing Canadian borders against illegal activity (counter-narcotics); fisheries protection; environmental surveillance; disaster relief; search and rescue; and counter-terrorism."[111] The policy even directed the transfer of counter-terrorism from the Royal Canadian Mounted Police Special Emergency Response team to their army's JTF-2 counter-terror unit.

To facilitate these changes in its domestic role, the Canadian Forces had to reorganize, specifically creating in its army structure, in 1993, a domestic operations staff at each of its four national regional headquarters. Subsequent to this, the Canadian Forces created a joint staff which has contributed to their ability to conduct domestic operations. With this new administrative structuring and changed legislation, "there are four main categories of services that the Canadian Forces provide in the domestic arena: those provided under acts, regulations, existing contracts, or agreements: (like the National Defense Act); services provided to other government departments (which in effect is assistance to the civil authority); the use of surplus defense capacity, and unspecified requests for services which are provided in the public interest."[112]

---

[109] Ibid.
[110] Ibid.
[111] Ibid., 144.
[112] Ibid.

The bottom line of the Canadian approach to the use of its Armed Forces in domestic

security is that their policy is more flexible than in the U.S.

> The military is not overburdened with legalities. The government
> accepts high reliance on military professionalism and training, and on
> an organization which has a higher loyalty than to elected officials.
> Although the political level may not always have known the details of
> civil-military relationships in domestic operations, in all cases they
> have understood that there are limits to the civil authorities' capability
> in terms of coordination, communications, mobility, organization,
> discipline, and force and have allowed the military to take over when
> the situation required it.[113]

The Canadians have placed such confidence in the professionalism of their armed forces,

along with their doctrine and method of training, that it can use them appropriately in

whatever capacity they are needed in defense of their nation and in support of civil

authorities.[114]

The United Kingdom Model

Like Israel, the United Kingdom (UK) has had extensive experience in domestic defense

issues, namely two decades of counter-terrorist campaigns in Northern Ireland. The UK is both a

unitary state and a parliamentary democracy. Its Parliament combines both executive and

legislative functions in one, making domestic policy and laws somewhat easier to establish.

Instead of state and local governments subordinated to the national governing body, Britain does

not delegate any powers to lower governments. In its place, the UK has forty-three police

constabularies, each operating independently, and commanded by its own Chief Constable. The

national government coordinates public safety and other domestic issues from a central office at

the National Reporting Center at Scotland Yard (London Police Headquarters) and through their

Home Office to the constabulary. The Constable claims all jurisdictions throughout his

---

[113] Ibid., 148-149.
[114] Howard, 131.

constabulary. The UK fire safety system mirrors the police constabulary system, making the coordination of either much more efficient, as well as less time intensive.[115]

At the highest level, the Home Office, headed by a Secretary, is overall responsible for internal domestic affairs in England and Wales, to include crisis and consequence management. The Home Office takes measures to promote individual and collective safety throughout UK communities. It also protects individual rights, and provides for protection and security of the public.[116] In the event of a crisis, the Home Secretary, or his deputy, chairs an interdepartmental cabinet working group to manage the incident. At the lowest level, the Chief Constable is in charge. The Ministry of Defense and military forces provide only advisory services on the scene, unless local police forces are unable to handle whatever is going on.[117] When the necessity exists for military forces to intervene in domestic affairs, British law dictates that authority for on-site command must pass by written document, establishing that responsibility has been passed from Chief Constable to a military commander. Once a situation is again manageable by local police forces, responsibility is again transferred by written document to the Constable.

Much like the Canadians, the British Ministry of Defense and armed forces are very active in the local community. "They help to support the police in Northern Ireland. They provide an expert capability throughout the United Kingdom to assist the civil authorities in dealing with explosive ordnance, from terrorist devices to bombs left over from previous wars. They are [also] ready to help during natural disasters."[118] In addition, the Royal Air Force and the Royal Navy both provide an on-call helicopter search and rescue capability within the UK, year-round. The Royal Navy also operates a Fishery Protection Squadron which does contract work for their Ministry of Agriculture Fisheries and Food. "It provides reassurance to fishermen and

---

[115] Ibid., 126.

[116] Her Majesty's Government, "The Home Office," [on-line]; available from http://www.homeoffice.gov.uk/; Internet; accessed 8 March 2002.

[117] Howard, 127.

[118] Ministry of Defence, "Defence in the Community," [on-line]; available from http://www.mod.uk/aboutus/factfiles/community.htm; Internet; accessed 8 March 2002.

enforces fisheries law within British Fisheries Limits, helping to conserve valuable and fragile fish stocks around Britain's coasts."[119]

The UK also uses their armed forces extensively for counter-drug operations. In that capacity, they help civil authorities stem the flow of illegal drugs, mostly by sea. In the last three years, the UK military has assisted in the seizure of illegal drugs with a street value of £2 Billion.[120] The British also keep a Special Air Service (SAS) team stationed permanently in London, responsible to Scotland Yard and the Home Secretary, to respond to national emergencies throughout the UK. This team, when employed, acts under strict guidelines against excessive use of force.[121]

In summary, though the UK form of government offers a unique advantage over the U.S. in handling domestic terrorism, more importantly, they have learned from extensive experience in counter-terror campaigns the proper use of military for such emergencies, coordination of operations between civilian and military entities, and the preeminence of unity of command.[122]

What They All Have to Offer

All three allied countries discussed above have unique portions of their domestic defense policy that may be beneficial as U.S. homeland security doctrine matures. For one, all three allies have clearly defined procedures for employment of military forces for domestic security matters. In Israel, the Homefront Command and military forces are the lead agency for internal crises, with authority over civilian agencies, in most cases, in times of war and peace. In Canada and the UK, the military and defense establishment plays a supporting role, however, when domestic crises occur, armed forces can assume lead agency either by written authorization or for specified time limits.

---

[119] Ibid.
[120] Ibid.
[121] Howard, 128.
[122] Ibid.

In the aftermath of the Cold War, many admire Israel's use of preemption and retribution as deterrence to terrorist activity. For this effort, Israel relies upon an extensive intelligence network, to include infiltration into suspect groups. Though the war on terror has shown some progress in this arena, U.S. law currently prohibits the wholesale sharing of military and civilian intelligence data.[123] The U.S. lacks such a robust, integrated intelligence network, however, the capability for such interagency cooperation is indeed possible. The thought behind such a policy would be for the U.S. to articulate to potential adversaries the immediate and massive retaliation that would accompany attacks to its homeland. This threat of preventive military action, many suggest, would provide a great deal of deterrence. Critics alternatively point out that this policy could fall short of its intent with a threat populated by non-state actors or even terrorists within one's own state.[124] The Israeli model also emphasizes the legitimacy of reserve forces to execute major portions of homeland defense. The Homefront Command is composed of ninety-seven percent reserve forces, yet, the Israelis are highly successful at deterring, preventing and, if necessary, responding to domestic crises.[125]

From the UK Model, U.S. policy makers can glean insights into interagency coordination during national crises. During an internal emergency, "…the Home Secretary is in charge and the others at the cabinet table are from the Foreign Office, the Ministry of Defense, the Police and Intelligence Services, and other ministries as necessary."[126] The Home Secretary assembles the appropriate cabinet members for the type and level of incident, and manages the response at the national level. The forty-three police constabularies are also plugged into coordination and response as necessary.

The Canadian Model also emphasizes the benefit of a seamless coordination and planning relationship between federal emergency agencies and defense agencies in handling national

---

[123] One exception to this is within JTF-6 and the U.S. counter-drug effort.
[124] Howard, 132-133.
[125] Israeli Defense Forces, "Homefront Command Organization," [on-line]; available from http://www.idf.il/english/organization/homefront/index.stm; Internet; accessed 1 March 2002.

emergencies. Canada achieved this through their post-1988 domestic revisions by creating the Emergency Preparedness Canada organization and subordinating it to their Department of National Defense, therefore linking the actions of the federal government with the provincial governments in creating joint material means and contingency plans to respond to their four types of national emergency.[127]

A final learning point is that all three countries rely on unity of command during times of crisis, and most have placed responsibility on their armed forces as the organization most trained and equipped to deal with domestic threats presented by today's current operational environment. "Israel, the UK, and Canada understand that military organizations intensively plan, organize, equip, and train for complex emergencies and that military commanders understand how to organize and coordinate multiple organizations for a common objective. Why not, they might ask their U.S. counterparts, make use of these distinctive capabilities in domestic emergencies?"[128]

---

126 Howard, 135.
127 Mahoney, 142 and 150.
128 Howard, 135

CHAPTER FIVE

RECOMMENDATIONS AND CONCLUSIONS

If Not Posse Comitatus, Then What?

This monograph contends that the *Posse Comitatus* Act is one of several problems that the Nation must come to grips with before an effective homeland defense policy and doctrine can operate in America. Moreover, while the heated debate continues over whether *Posse Comitatus* statutes are still truly a "great bulwark in our democratic society," this monograph has argued that given the current focus of national security documents (such as the NSS, NMS, and the 2001 QDR), a greater than twenty-year precedent of military employment in the War on Drugs, commensurate involvement in other domestic crises, and the current threat environment post-September 11, 2001, that the *Posse Comitatus* Act is at best a relic greatly in need of revision.

The *Posse Comitatus* Act hinders the full employment of DOD assets in the domestic environment necessary to bring success in the homeland defense effort. *Posse Comitatus* statutes, as interpreted in today's environment, are confusing and present too many opportunities for misinterpretation, both for lawmakers and for military commanders on the ground. The *Posse Comitatus* Act is rooted in the historic fear of standing armies in America, which may still have some validity in the foundation of the American democracy, but which greatly conflicts with the domestic environment which America is faced with today. And the *Posse Comitatus* Act has been weakened (and circumvented) through numerous legislation in the past twenty years that, in effect, the statute is already proven void.

Homeland Security is not a new subject, especially in this age of WMD proliferation and the escalation of terror attacks on the U.S. homeland. There have been many excellent ideas published through discussion papers, expressed at conferences, in think tanks, amongst Congressional caucuses, and between national security strategists over the past several years.

With the Nation at war, several recommendations emerge with an eye toward providing better domestic security overall, given the current threat, and the right federal organization—with or without *Posse Comitatus.*

First, in regards to whether the regular Armed Forces (and specifically the active Army) should play a more significant role in the homeland security mission, the facts are clear that the Nation must now maintain a higher measure of readiness in regards to terrorism. No single federal agency can handle the immense tasks inclusive of defense of the U.S. homeland alone. While the state and federally deployed National Guard forces have provided the immediate layer of safety required to return the country to a closer form of normalcy, pre-September 11, 2001, the current OPTEMPO of deployment of those specific forces cannot be maintained forever. For one, such a high deployment OPTEMPO of the Nation's Guard forces will eventually degrade their own warfighting abilities, as well as limit the Commander-in-Chief's options for major theater war. Second, those forces will also be spread too thin to respond to state emergencies. In regards to employment of regular troops, this document has previously detailed the danger in over reliance on the active military for domestic protection, which may diminish the military's capability to promote U.S. foreign policy and win the Nation's wars. Therefore, it would not be prudent to divert active duty forces from the missions already on each respective Service's plate.

A viable solution would be for the Armed Forces, specifically the Army, to expand, to facilitate the homeland defense requirement that will be necessary for the foreseeable future. Such action could be justified inclusive of the Army's responsibilities within DOD as executive agent for homeland security. The ongoing Army transformation from a Legacy, to Interim, and future Objective Force already provides the impetus for change. As part of the Army Transformation efforts, this organizational alternative would feature an Objective Force with a bifurcated structure: one branch would include expeditionary forces with force projection priorities to fulfill the national engagement strategy; the other branch would include "homeland defense forces" with necessary capabilities for immediate employment in the War on Terrorism

46

and the Nation's homeland defense effort. The advantage of having dedicated homeland defense forces is that if necessary, they can be created under legislation similar to the National Guard (Title 32), which does not prohibit their employment in law enforcement roles in defense of the Nation, therefore staying in compliance with the *Posse Comitatus* Act.

A FAS test examination of this alternative yields mixed results. First, as demonstrated, the weakening of the *Posse Comitatus* Act over the years suggests that revision of the Act would be almost seamless, considering the manner and frequency in which troops are employed domestically today. The use of dedicated homeland defense forces is a feasible option because with or without *Posse Comitatus*, and combined with other initiatives, it provides better defense of the homeland. Both the acceptability and suitability of such an option, however, would trigger much debate. Many in the country perhaps now accept the fact that operations necessary for limiting potential terrorist freedom of action in the U.S. (which in turn accomplishes the goal of the War on Terror by preventing, eliminating, and deterring future terrorist activity), also impinges upon U.S. citizens' personal freedoms. In this manner, the country at large may accept the regular employment of troops in the domestic arena as a necessary evil to defeat terrorism, however, in view of America's historic fear of regular forces in domestic roles, this matter would have to be addressed clearly and directly by the Nation's leaders.[129] In like manner, the addition of dedicated homeland defense forces would be a suitable solution in that it potentially provides for better defense of the homeland, but without revision of other domestic security matters, including interagency coordination, command and control, and unity of command, additional troops alone will not accomplish the desired effect. If this alternative is to work, then, other security measures must accompany it.

Chief among these other recommended measures is the revision of the National Security Act of 1947. The National Security Act created much of the U.S. security structure today, to include the Department of Defense, Air Force, Central Intelligence Agency, and the National

Security Council. Optimized for fighting the Cold War, the Act no longer addresses America's role as superpower, does not recognize the current global security environment, the proliferation of WMD, and does not address the rogue nations, failed states, and non-state behavior that dominate the list of potential security threats to the U.S. and her allies.[130] In addition to addressing the structure of interagency efforts, this new Act must provide for a seamless integration of intelligence sources for domestic security purposes. Like JTF-6, and much like the IDF and Homefront Command in Israel, U.S. intelligence sources must become robust and integrated. Future domestic defense will require multi-agency, multi-dimensional, and even coalition based intelligence systems that possess the ability to track, locate, and possible destroy terrorist cells and other security threats to national sovereignty. Information from law enforcement, regulatory, financial, intelligence and military sources must all filter into actionable intelligence.[131]

A natural adjunct to the revision of the 1947 National Securities Act is the creation of a Homeland Security Command with commensurate CINC structure and staff. In previous years such an organization has been referred to as "Americom," or "Homeland Defense Command." One version of command structure organizes the entire Army for war. The 1st and 5th U.S. Armies would become operational headquarters. The U.S. would be divided into two commands, Joint Area of Operation (JOA) East and West, each with a synchronized, joint and interagency staff facilitated by the Army. The two commands would be subordinate to the newly created JTF-Civil Support (Homeland Security Command HQ), and/or Headquarters Joint Forces Command. The Army Operational headquarters would serve as JTF headquarters, with the capability to serve as a Joint Force Land Component Command, and Army Service Component Command for operations within the United States and its possessions. Additionally, each

---

[129] William J. Miller et. al, 9.

[130] Howard, 99 and 108-109. See also William A. Navas, Jr., "The National Security Act of 2002," in *Organizing for National Security*, Douglas T. Stuart, ed. (Carlisle Barracks, PA: Strategic Studies Institute, 2000), 231-244.

command would assume responsibility for all installations and Army related operations within their defined JOAs. The interagency integration mechanism within each JOA would incorporate the host of local, state and federal agencies necessary to coordinate and execute a more transparent homeland defense program at every level, to include: local law enforcement, FEMA, FBI, DIA, DOT, CIA, FAA, ATF, HHS, CDC, INS, DOS, and OHS.[132] Recently, national media sources have announced a Pentagon plan for a new four-star billet that would oversee some future version of a "Homeland Command" with an assigned CINC-dom in the very near term. The organization for such a command is undisclosed at present, except to mention that the Secretary of Defense desires to create a new command rather than load additional responsibilities on an existing one.[133]

Many have applauded the creation of the cabinet-level position for homeland security. In the same breath, others have criticized that this high level executive, with ready access to the President (like the former "drug czar"), has little coordinating power, a small staff, and oversight over a large budget, but not enough control over the many agencies that exhaust those funds in the Nation's homeland security effort.[134] The current administration must empower the current Director of the Office of Homeland Security with "super-agency" powers, continued ready access to Congress and the President, and a greater degree of control over the nation's domestic defense budget. Adhering to the tenets of civilian control, the "super-empowered" Director of OHS must also be *the* unifying entity in the entire homeland security effort.

The Bush administration should review the domestic policies of those U.S. allies with proven success against domestic violence and terrorism, to include the three mentioned in this monograph. Each of the democracies discussed—Israel, Canada, and the UK—adhere to civilian

---

[131] William J. Miller, et al., 1.

[132] William J. Miller, "Organizing for Combat," (Concept paper, Command and General Staff College-School of Advanced Military Studies, 2001), 1.

[133] Graham Bradley, "Pentagon Plans New Command for U.S.," [online]; available from http://www.washington.com/ac2/wp-dyn/A42765-2002Jan26; Internet; accessed 9 March 2002.

[134] Paul C. Light, "Clout Is Key; Post Lacks It," *USA Today*, 9 October 2001, 14.

control of the military, yet have government structures that do not require restricting legislation like *Posse Comitatus*. Each of these states also makes very effective use of their armed forces for employment in domestic security needs.[135] One Israeli organizational practice deserving study is how Israel's Homefront Command succeeds in deterring, preventing, and responding to domestic threats when ninety-seven percent of the organization consists of reserve forces. The U.S. must explore better organization and employment of its reserve and National Guard forces for the long-term effort against terrorism. And as previously argued, DOD must explore the option of creating active or reserve homeland divisions or brigades which could fulfill explicit homeland defense-type missions under the new Homeland Defense Command.

Final Word

Without doubt, the advent of the current operating environment and the Nation's current "whatever it takes" attitude toward collective safety and protection against terrorism in America has made *Posse Comitatus* all but void. On September 11, 2001, the world changed as we know it. Most Americans realize this. The liberty America once new is no longer available, and the freedom that Americans maintain in the future will not come as freely as before.

Homeland Security is perhaps the most difficult and important mission the U.S. will undertake since World War II. As such, it must maximize all of the Nation's sources of power domestically and abroad; it must be combined arms, joint, interagency, coalition and multi-dimensional in nature in order to succeed in the elimination, prevention and deterrence of terror at home and in the world. The *Posse Comitatus* Act hinders the full cooperation and flexible integration of DOD assets with federal agencies to affect the War on terror in the domestic environment. As demonstrated in the War on Drugs, the military may be the best option domestically in this endeavor in the employment of troops, protection of critical infrastructure, and as lead agency for counter-terrorism. The government must explore this as a viable option.

---

[135] Howard, 140.

The U.S. military is a much more professional force today than it was in the late eighteenth century. Professional armies serve their country and their flag. The Armed Forces of the U.S. are here to serve America today, not usurp the authority given it to protect the Nation, defend her borders and win the Nation's war. As servants of the Nation, the Armed Forces must answer the Nation's call to provide for the common defense and promote the general welfare. Radical change is needed in America's domestic security. Several options exist; the government must continue to remain sensitive to Nation's foundation, and the traditional role of military organizations in a democratic society. At the same time, where America's foundational tenets conflict with the reality of today, our method of providing for the common defense and maintaining the American way of life must give way to change.

BIBLIOGRAPHY

Books

Carter, Ashton B., John M. Deutch, and Philip D. Zelikow. *Catastrophic Terrorism: Elements of a National Policy*. Cambridge, Mass.: Harvard University Press, 1988b.

Robert W. Coakley. *The Role of Federal Military Forces in Domestic Disorders, 1789-1878*. Washington, DC: U.S. Government Printing Office, 1988.

Kohn, Richard H. *Eagle and Sword: The Beginnings of the Military Establishment in America*. New York, NY: The Free Press, 1975.

Larson, Eric V. and John E. Peters. *Preparing the U.S. Army for Homeland Security: Concepts, Issues and Options*. Santa Monica, CA: RAND, 2001.

Laurie, Clayton D. and Ronald H. Cole. *The Role of Federal Military Forces in Domestic Disorders 1877-1945*. Washington, DC: U.S. Government Printing Office, 1997.

Lesser, Ian O. et al. *Countering the New Terrorism*. Santa Monica, CA: RAND, 2001.

Manwaring, Max G. Editor. *"...to insure domestic Tranquility, provide for the common defense..."*. Carlisle Barracks, PA: Strategic Studies Institute, 2000.

Millet, Allan R. and Peter Maslowski. *For the Common Defense: A Military History of the United States of America*. New York, NY: The Free Press, 1994.

Wright, Robert K., Jr. and Morris J. MacGregor, Jr. eds. *Soldier-Statesmen of the Constitution*. Washington, DC: Center of Military History, United States Army, 1987.

Articles

Baker, Bonnie. "The Origins of the Posse Comitatus." At www.airpower.maxwell.af.mil/ Chronicles/cc/baker1/html. November 1, 1999.

Bender, Bryan. "U.S. DOD Clamps Down on Threats over the Internet." *Jane's Defence Weekly*, Vol. 32, No. 9, September 1, 1999.

Betts, Richard K. "Analysis, War, and Decision: Why Intelligence Failures Are Inevitable." *World Politics*, Vol. 31, No. 1, October 1978, pp. 61-89.

Byrne, Sean J. "Defending Sovereignty: Domestic Operations and Legal Precedents." *Military Review,* March/April 1999.

Castelli, Christopher J. "Homeland Terrorism, More Kosovos Ahead, Security Panel Warns." *Inside the Navy*. August 9, 1999, p. 1.

Cohen, William S. "Preparing for a Grave New World." *Washington Post*. July 26, 1999, p. A19.

Cooper, Jerry. "The Posse Comitatus Act." in John Whiteclay Chambers, II ed., *The Oxford Companion to American Military History,* 1999, pp. 555-556.

Davis, Ted. "Evaluating National Security Strategy and National Military Strategy." Reprinted in US Army Command and General Staff College, C500 *Fundamentals of Operational Warfighting, L1-E1,2.* Fort Leavenworth: USACGSC, August 2000.

Gal-Or, Noemi. "Countering Terrorism in Israel," in David A. Charters, ed., *The Deadly Sin of Terrorism: Its Effects on Democracy and Civil Liberty in Six Countries.* Westport, CT, Centre for Conflict Studies, University of New Brunswick, 1994.

Garamone, Jim. "DOD Examines Joint Task Force Concept for Civil Support." American Forces Information Service, AugU.S.t 17, 1999, at http://www.defenselink.nil/news/Aug1999/n0081799_9908175.html.

_____. "Senate Grills Myers on Homeland Defense, Transformation." *DefenseLink*, September, 15, 2001, at http://www.defenselink.mil/cgi-bin/dlprint.cgi.

Graham, Bradley. "Pentagon Plans Domestic Terror Team; Critics Fear Too Much Military Interference in Civilian Emergency Response." *Washington Post*, February 1, 1999, p. A2.

Grange, David L., and Rodney L. Johnson. "Forgotten Mission: Military Support to the Nation." *Joint Forces Quarterly*, No. 15, Spring 1997, pp. 108-115.

Holmes, H. Allen. "Domestic Preparedness: U.S. Reponses Need Tuning." *Defense Viewpoint*, Vol. 13, No. 33, March 26, 1998, p. 5. at http://www.defenselink.mil/speeches/1998/s19980326-holmas.html.

Lee, Debra R. "Protecting Americans at Home." *Defense Link*, March, 19, 1998, p. 2. at http://www.defenselink.mil/other_info/deblee.html.

Miller, Judith, and William J. Broad. "Clinton Describes Terrorism Threat for 21st Century." *New York Times*, January 22, 1999.

MSNBC. "Does U.S. Need Anti-Terror Troops? Pentagon, FEMA at Odds over Plans Rose, Gideon. "It Could Happen Here—Facing the New Terrorism." *Foreign Affairs*, March-April, 1999, p. 135.

Sprinzak, Ehud. "Terrorism, Real or Imagined—What is the Real Threat, WMC or Car Bombs?" *Washington Post*. August 19, 1998, p. A21.

"The Homefront is Prepared." *Israel Wire*, December 18, 1998, at http://www.israelwire.com/lra/981218/9812184.html.

"Tiananmen Square, Waco, and Posse Comitatus." AmeriRoots, October 16, 2001, at http://www.ameriroots.com/issues/tiananmen_waco.html.

Weiss, Aaron. "When Terror Strikes, Who Should Respond?" *Parameters*, Autumn 2001, pp. 117-33.

Thesis, Monographs and Reports

Allison, Graham, Matthew Bunn, Ashton Carter, John Deutch, Richard Falkenrath, John Holdren,

Robert Newman, and Joe Nye. "Defending the United States Against Weapons of Mass Destruction." Unpublished memorandum to the U.S. Senate, June 2, 1997, at http://ksgnotes1.harvard.eud/BCSIA/Library.nsf/wwwdocsname/ defend U.S..

American Civil Liberties Union. "ACLU Says Broad New Anti-Terrorism Measure Could Encroach on Americans' Rights," ACLU news release, January 25, 1999, at http://www.aclu.org/news/1999/n012599 a.html.

Anderson, Donnie P. *The Army's Commitment to Supporting the Homeland Security Chemical, Biological, Radiological, Nuclear, and High-Yield Explosive Weapon Terrorist Threat: Can the Reserve Components Meet the Requirement by Themselves?* Carlisle Barracks, PA: U.S. Army War College, 2001.

Benson, Nolon J., Jr. *The Posse Comitatus Act: Is There a Need for Change?* Carlisle Barracks, PA: U.S. Army War College, 1998.

Blake, Jeffrey D. "Terrorism and the Military's role in Domestic Crisis Management: Background and Issues for Congress." Congressional Research Service, April 19, 2001, at http://www.fas.org/irp/crs/RL30928.pdf.

Demarest, Geoffrey. "The Overlap of Military and Police in Latin America." *Foreign Military Studies Office Publications.* April, 1995.

Echevarria II, Antulio J. *The Army and Homeland Security: A Strategic Perspective.* Carlisle Barracks, PA: Strategic Studies Institute, March 2001.

Engdahl, David E. *Soldiers, Riots, and Revolution: The Law and History of Military Troops in Civil Disorders.* 57 Iowa Law Rev. 1, October 1971.

Grant, T. J. "Training on Rules of Engagement in Domestic Operations." Unpublished paper, Canadian Defense College, at http://www.cfcsc.dnd.ca/irc/amsc/amsc1/014.html, p. 1.

Ikle, Fred C. *Defending the U.S. Homeland: Strategic and Legal Issues for DOD and the Armed Services.* Washington, D.C.: Center for Strategic and International Studies, January 1999.

Kelly, Terrence. "An Organizational Framework for Homeland Defense." *Parameters*, Autumn 2001, pp. 105-16.

Lujan, Thomas R. "Legal Aspects of Domestic Employment of the Army." *Parameters*, Autumn 1997, pp. 82-97.

Maloney, Sean M. "Domestic Operations: The Canadian Approach." *Parameters*, Autumn 1997, p. 143.

Navas, William A., Jr. "The National Security Act of 2002," in *Organizing for National Security*, Douglas T. Stuart, Editor. Carlisle Barracks, PA: Strategic Studies Institute, 2000, 231-244.

Miller, Steven L. *The Military, Domestic Law Enforcement, and Posse Comitatus: A Time for Change.* Maxwell Air Force Base, AL: Air Command and Staff College, April 2000.

Miller, William, J., Sven Erichsen, and Jeffery K. Toomer. *Homeland Security: A Campaign Framework*. Unpublished Concept Paper. Command and General Staff College-School of Advanced Military Studies, 2001.

Miller, William, J. *Organizing for Combat*. Unpublished Concept Paper. Command and General Staff College-School of Advanced Military Studies, 2001.

"Operations Other than War Volume II—Disaster Assistance." *Center for Army Lessons Learned Newsletter*, no. 93-6, October 1993, p. IX 2.

Stevens, Paul Schott. *U.S. Armed Forces and Homeland Defense: The Legal Framework*. Washington, D.C.: Center for Strategic and International Studies. October 2001.

Tribelcock, Craig T. *Posse Comitatus.—Has the Posse Outlived Its Purpose?* Washington, D.C.: Center for Strategic and International Studies, April 2000.

_____. "The Myth of Posse Comitatus." *Journal of Homeland Defense*, October 27, 2000, at www.homelanddefense.org.

Primary Sources

Department of the Army. *Domestic Disaster Assistance: A Primer for Attorneys*. The Judge Advocate General's School, Center for Law and Military Operations, Charlottesville, VA: undated.

_____. *Army Strategic Planning Guidance*, Washington, D.C., April 16, 1999.

_____. *DA Pam 550-25, Israel: A Country Study*. Washington, D.C., 1988.

Department of Defense. *Proliferation Threat and Response*. Washington, D.C.: 1996.

_____. *Domestic Preparedness Program in the Defense Against Weapons of Mass Destruction*. Washington, D.C., May 1, 1997, at http://www.defenselink.mil/pubs/domestic/ index.html.

_____. *DOD Directive 3025.1*, Military Support to Civil Authorities (MSCA), January 20, 1993.

_____. *DOD Directive 3025.12*, Military Assistance for Civil Disturbances (MACDIS), February 4, 1994.

_____. *DOD Directive 3025.15*, Military Assistance to Civil Authorities (MACA), January 15, 1997.

_____. Quadrennial Defense Review Report. Washington, D.C.: September 2001.

Department of Defense Tiger Team. *Department of Defense Plan for Integrating National Guard and Reserve Component Support for Response to Attacks Using Weapons of Mass Destruction*. Washington, D.C., January 1998, at http://www.defenselink.nil/pubs/ wmdresponse/.

Federal Bureau of Investigation. *Terrorism in the United States*. Various years.

Federal Emergency Management Agency. *Introduction to the Basic Plan of the Federal Response Plan.* April 1999a at http://www.fas.org/irp/offdocs/pdd39_frp.htm.

General Accounting Office. *Combating Terrorism: Use of National Guard Response Teams Is Unclear.* Washington, D.C.: GAO/NSIAD-99-151, June 1999.

Joint Chiefs of Staff. *Shape, Respond, and Prepare Now: A Military Strategy for a New Era.* Washington, D.C.: 1997.

_____. Joint Pub 3.0, *Doctrine for Joint Operations*, September 10, 2001.

National Defense Panel. *Transforming Defense: National Security in the 21st Century.* Washington, D.C.: December, 1997.

Office of the Secretary of Defense. *Proliferation: Threat and Response.* Washington, D.C.: Government Printing Office, January 2001.

President's Commission on Critical Infrastructure Protection. *Critical Foundations: Protecting America's Infrastructures.* Washington, D.C.: October, 1997.

The White House. PDD-39, "U.S. Policy on Counterterrorism." June 21, 1995 at http://www.fas.org/irp/offdocs/pdd39.htm.

_____. PDD-62, "Protecting Against Unconventional Threats to the Homeland and Americans Overseas." May 22, 1998.

_____. PDD-63, "The Clinton Administration's Policy on Critical Infrastructure Protection." May 1998.

_____. *A National Security Strategy for a Global Age.* Washington, D.C.: December 2000.

Title 10 U.S. Code, Sections 371-382, Military Support to Civilian Law Enforcement Agencies.

Title 18 U.S. Code, Section 1385, The Posse Comitatus Act.

www.ingramcontent.com/pod-product-compliance
Lightning Source LLC
Chambersburg PA
CBHW080545290526
45790CB00006B/2560